SCRAPS
Carla Mellor

SCRAPS
Carla Mellor

All rights reserved. No part of this book may be reproduced, stored in a retrieval system or transmitted in any form or by any means electronic, mechanical, photocopying, recording or otherwise, without the prior permission of the publisher.

ISBN 978-1903110867

First published in this edition 2021 by Wrecking Ball Press.

Copyright: Carla Mellor

Cover illustration: Gemma Sargent

All rights reserved.

For Tash, who I can never quite put into words.

Big thanks to Toria Garbutt for being my mentor, and my friend. Special thanks also to Louise Fazackerley, Kirsty Taylor, Roy, Joe West, Keiron Higgins and all the poets at the Old Courts in Wigan for their ongoing support.

CONTENT

ADULTING 9
SUNDAY EVENINGS 11
LIGHTHOUSE 12
THERE'S A JUNKIE IN OUR KITCHEN 14
NETTO BASHER 16
UNDER THE CARPET 20
NEW SHOES 23
SCRAPS 25
CIDER KING 27
FAG BREAK 29
HALF A CAN CARLA 32
FAIRYTALES AND UNWANTED MAIL 35
POVERTY TOURISM 38
LIVE-IN-TOURIST 39
LITTLE MOSHER 42
SUNSHINE 43
SUITS 45
EMOTIONAL HOARDER 49
ANXIETY 51
SISTER 53
NEURODIVERSITY 54
SELF-CARE 58
DAYS 59
TOO BUSY LISTENING 62
SIDE BY SIDE 63
KARAOKE GRANDAD: SIDE A 64
KARAOKE GRANDAD: SIDE B 67
SPOONS 69
BROKEN BISCUITS 70
WE ARE ALL FRAGMENTS OF SOMEBODY ELSE ... 71

ADULTING

From muddy knees
and climbing trees
to paying fines
and settling fees

From digging dirt
and mucky shirts
to getting up
to go to work

From rubber bands
and castles of sand
to interest rates
on ninety grand

From running noses
to picking roses
to surfing sofas
and recommended doses

From grazed elbows
to there she goes
to all your worries
all your woes

From playing tag
to smoking fags
to watch it sag
to withered hag

From crawl
to walk
and coo
to talk

From knowing nothing
to knowing it all
to not knowing
what it's all for

SUNDAY EVENINGS

An exotic looking house plant in a swan shaped vase,
a fat back TV and a VCR

Sitting on't floor and watching cartoons
on a heavily patterned carpet, fit for a Wetherspoons

Videos in sleeves that looked like books,
weak orange squash in plastic cups

Textured wallpaper and curtain pelmets,
sitting in front of't fire when yer hair's wet

from its weekly wash on a Sunday evening,
with *last of the summer wines* on't TV screen

and a belly full of Sunday roast,
it's those Sunday evenings that I miss the most

LIGHTHOUSE

First one to see the lighthouse wins
fuck all
other than to be
the first one to see the lighthouse

I always have to sit
in the middle
a human arm rest
elbows fly into me
as my sister turns the page of her magazine
and my brother button bashes his game boy

The motorway is an endless stretch
of lights whizzing by
above my head
out the corner of my eye

I'm so small and
they seem so high
like stars falling
from the sky

Back roads
loop and wind
and my siblings take it in turns
to fold
and fall
and lean
into me
at every bend

one right
one left
I am middle ground

Funny how we grew
and yet it remains this way
a little bit different
but mostly the same

THERE'S A JUNKIE IN OUR KITCHEN

There's a junkie in our bathroom
he's stood over the sink
wide eyes on't running water
he doesn't even blink

He's mumbling to himself
his hands are proper shaking
been washing 'em so long
his nails have started flaking

There's a junkie in our kitchen
pacing up and down
he just won't stand still
fag hangin' out of his mouth

There's a junkie in our living room
on our blue chenille settee
staring at the ringing house phone
chewing holes in his jumper sleeve

There's a junkie in our garden
he let me comb his hair
I put some clips and bows in it
and he let me leave them there

There were a junkie in our house
we were playing hide and seek
but he's nowhere to be found
and I've been looking now for weeks

I ask about the junkie
they just say he's gone away
I don't know why or where
I hope he'll come back some day

There's no junkie in our house now
to play fun games with me
fondly call me 'ratbag'
and sit down with us for tea

There's a man at my front door
he's familiar to me
he looks just like the junkie did
but different, older, clean

NETTO BASHER

Looking up
at Houghton Towers
I thought they looked
like New York skyscrapers
and that the electricity pylon
up on't moors
that I could see
from my bedroom window
was so so far away
that it must be the Eiffel Tower
'cause I was small enough for't whole world
to fit into Sowerby Bridge

I remember it in colours
mostly green and grey
we'd play on the grassy roundabout
in the middle of the road all day
where amongst crisp packets and white dog poo
dandelions bloomed
stubborn weeds
wit' deepest roots

And just like them
we were weeds not flowers
popping up in terraces
and high-rise towers
we sprung up
here and there
with dirty faces and

knotted hair
us kids on't street
were everywhere

Running wild down ginnels
loitering outside the offy
hanging out in car parks
getting proper gobby

Because the park near us
well it wasn't even that
it was one swing set
on a concrete slab
and the seats were always
wrapped round t'frame
nothing to do but
graffiti yer name
on't big wooden fence
that boxed us all inside
a gaping hole in't floor
from where a rusted metal roundabout
used to reside

Just another forgotten
Northern town
where mills and factories
all shut down
and the only thing that was made there in the nineties
was us

Multiplying faster than
dandelion seeds
Blooming up as baby boomers
had more kids
than they could feed

Hand me downs
and leaving the bath water in
for yer sister
brother
father
mother
that bloke down't street
any old bugger

Sitting on the cellar roof
after school
and shouting
"mam provvy man is ere"
and she'd correct me
"it's provident lass,
don't be crass"
as she handed the loan shark
her hard-earned brass
pretending like we weren't
textbook working class

For school she'd take a marker pen
to the back of my break time crisps
to stop that Netto scotty dog
on that yellow rectangle of his
taunting me
and if she ever forgot
those kids who proudly shovelled quavers and skips
into their privileged little gobs
would spit crumbs at me as they mouthed
"Povvo, povvo, yer mam shops at Netto"

UNDER THE CARPET

Just lift up
the corners
of the rug
take that great big brush
and sweep it all
under the carpet
there's no need
to talk about it

what will the neighbours think?
what will they say?
Just keep my clothes clean
and food in my belly
and we'll all sit around
and just stare
at the telly

there's no need for confrontation
or even any conversation
let's just be like ships that pass in the night
even in the day
It's fine
It's okay

Nobody died
Nearly but not quite
It doesn't warrant flowers
or cards
or time to grieve

you can't mourn someone
who is still alive
who only wanted to leave
this life
there's no need
for therapy
just put the kettle on
and have a cup of tea

We don't need to talk about it
we just need to put it aside
pretend it never happened
and get on with our lives

If there's nowt to say about the weather
or what's for tea
we'll sit in silence
and smile politely

You might comment on
the time of day
and the things that I need
to tidy away
you won't ask about
how I feel
there's no need for that
It's far too real

We don't do that here
in our little Northern town
in this little terraced house
where the carpets are always hoovered
and the windows are always clean
and there's never any dirt or dust
and the bins
are always
always
out
on
time

NEW SHOES

I got new trainers every time
my cousin sized up
washing powder on an old toothbrush
trying to cover the scuffs

They were Fila or Kappa
sometimes Umbro
they were't only thing
I had with a proper logo

Until her feet wouldn't stop growing
and her shoes were no use
I'd need ten pairs of socks
and they'd still be too loose

Me Mam took me to Sports Direct
with a budget of thirty quid
to get me some trainers
the ones with the tick

They didn't have my size
a six and a half
at the allocated price
so I got a size five

I told her they fit

Must be better sizing I said
with proper branded shoes
I walked up and down the shop
to prove it were true

I scrunched my toes
throughout year nine
I hobbled for a whole year
and I took it in my stride
I couldn't feel my toes
as I shuffled about with pride

all for that little blue tick

and the compliments I got
on my nice new kicks

SCRAPS

Apron on
hair pulled back
peeling spuds
right from the sack

Oil
coats
everything
and
everything
sticks
to
oil

Not much that can't be
battered
buttered
drenched in vinegar
radio crackles
from the grease
In the speaker
for two pound fifty an hour
this is where she spends
her weekends

Her varnished fingers
trace sodium hearts
on the metal counter
'make a wish!'

She blows the grains
her distorted reflection is
makeup melting off
and
teenage pimples
protruding
through her
three ninety-nine market slap

Wage in a brown envelope and
a free bag of scraps to take away
for the girl who dreams
of flying away
like the seagulls could
but they don't, they stay

Hard to muster the courage
to be brave enough to escape
when even something with wings
chooses to stay

CIDER KING

You are the only boy
whose hoody I've ever,
will ever,
steal

Fag burns badly stitched
in't wrong coloured thread
in a poor attempt to hide
the things we never wanted
our mothers
to learn about us

You could chug
a bottle of white star
anywhere
round the back of Welly club
before pop and crisp
emo rock night

FUCK YOU I WON'T DO WHAT YOU TELL ME

we were little anarchists
headbanging all night
chain smoking in fingerless gloves
on't bus home by nine

You
in black
and black

and black
and green
Chuck Taylor's
Me
shivering in a skirt
I made out of safety pins
and net curtains

Us on Wiv beach
or market stalls
or on't skate park
where you'd
watch me fall
drunkenly adamant
that I knew how to skateboard
In jeans so tight I could barely breathe
them ones I nicked
from't top of Prinny Quay

Justified by treating us both
at Huckleberry Finns
to two portions of chips and cheese
and booze
and fags
and resin
that we couldn't even roll

FAG BREAK

Hustled round t'back of t'lecky shed
at first break of the day
in hindsight not very safe,
mixing electricity with flames

You're not a mosher here
or an emo or a chav
we put all that aside
to come and have a fag

There's goths lending lighters
to lads wearing sovereigns
and orange faced lasses
who date lads with Citroen Saxo's
saving last drags for
that lass wi't bull ring in her nose

And if you've not got owt to smoke
you can buy yourself a single
just not the first one of the pack
'cause that one,
that's your lucky fag
and
it's ritual to take that out
and turn it round
and put it back
and smoke it last

But you can buy one of the other nine
from someone's
two pound thirty
ten pack

Behind the shed
everyone's a smoker
it's the only label here
for twenty minutes of the day
you can ask a chav to buy a fag
and they won't call you
mosher
weird
emo
goth
gay

You can banter and barter
without getting bullied
learn more about doing deals
then you would in business studies

Entrepreneurs in the making
it's ours for the taking

"I'll give you 30p mate
but only for a straight
I don't want no doley rolly
I want a proper tailor made

not a hand rolled
lump of
Amber Leaf
imported in
from Tenerife
enclosed in those
cheap thick skins
from't bargain bin
of Poundland

Teenagers don't buy bacci
'cause it don't look cool to smoke it
bet you robbed if off yer Mam or Dad
and now you can't even offload it
'cause it looks like
Stevie Wonder rolled it
and it's still wet from your spit
I aren't giving you thirty pence for that pal
I'll give you ten
but that's it"

HALF A CAN CARLA

Half a can Carla
they called me
but I disagreed
look here
see

It were Special Brew
it's fucking lethal
washed down with
three shots of some liqueur
that smelt like peach
and taste like treacle

Let's not forget all the
knock off L and Bs
me mates Mam
had sold us cheap

In dodgy packaging
flecked with brown
where they'd got wet
and then dried out

What were even in 'em
I couldn't really say
they were rancid but
the nicci rush were ace

They hurt to smoke
like inhaling glass
but we only paid
two quid a pack

They smelt like fish
but then so did
the
whole
of
that
fucking
town

So we sucked in mould
drank stolen beer
on't park, on't beach, on
North End pier

And I got this nickname
half a can Carla

I'd always wanted a nickname
but this one weren't cool
and I got stuck with it
for't last three years of school

But I remember the event well
'cause I wasn't that smashed
I just pretended I was
'cause there were this lass

I wanted so badly
to hold her hand
as I sat there sipping
half of my can

So I pretended to fall over drunk
so she'd help me stay upright
'cause
half a can Carla
well, it were better than
'dyke'

FAIRYTALES AND UNWANTED MAIL

Penned in
by red bricks
dilapidated fences
overgrown gardens

Rising bus fares
keep 'em at bay
walk for miles
or suck it up and stay
'cause
"far far away"
is nowt but a
bed time story
at the end
of the day

Read to bairns in
box room
bunk beds
textured wallpaper
damp and peeling
artex patterns
up on't ceiling
thinning carpets
and the streetlight seeps
where charity shop curtains
don't quite meet

Weights rest heavy
on Mam's fragile shoulders
frail from a diet of
beans on toast and
9p noodles
pennies pinched
for t'gas meter
and new school shoes

Fairytales fill
little hearts
wi' hope but
Mams need
their own
to cope

and
dream

Of a week in Spain
all inclusive
but swim only in
second-hand bathwater and
leaky washer suds

eat nothing
but spuds

and
sunbathe
under a brown parasol of
final notice
last chance
envelopes

POVERTY TOURISM
First published in Jarg Zine issue 3

Poverty tourism photo shoots
down back alleys
of streets you don't live down
have never played tig down
or had a crafty cig down

Snaps of high-rise tower blocks
that you've never had to climb all't stairs of
'cause the lift ain't working
again

Fashion shoots posed by graffitied doors
that you've never opened
never rang the half melted, fag burnt intercom of
heard the click clack of the door
as yer buzzed in
'cause you've never even been in

Instead you take scenic snaps of balcony bunting
int' form of washing hanging out to dry
a colourful backdrop
on a cold grey sky

You'll post it on Instagram
#urban #street
then you'll get in yer car
and drive home for yer tea

LIVE-IN-TOURIST

In London I dreamt
of smashing glass ceilings,
Instead with little balance
and poor concentration
I smashed glasses,
poured pints
and chucked drunks t'pavement

Spent the last of the recession
learning Cockney rhyming slang,
dialled down my Yorkshire accent
just so punters could understand

What I said
when I said

"Slow down on the vodka,
you've had one too many love"

and i've had enough
of not making much
at all
of being left
with fuck all
after paying my way

Hadn't realised when I arrived,
eager and naive,
that this city would

beat me,
deflate
and defeat me,
demand so much,
consume me,
deplete me,
become me

Water me down
and dilute me

Plum-mouthed silver spooners
driving round in fancy cars,
and my Bachelors of Arts
landed me straight behind the bar

It became my place of comfort,
as close to home as I could get
without a train journey
that cost a weeks worth of rent
or a megabus
with four hours gone, lost, spent

It became my happy place,
my safe space
nestled between fancy bars
that I couldn't afford to frequent,
just another live-in tourist
struggling to pay their rent

Landmarks, buses, statues, parks
all merged into one
and i'd have traded them all
just for a song

Sung
badly

A familiar karaoke classic
in that distinctive
Yorkshire accent
H's dropped
And O's
rolled round
I'd swap the city in an instant
just for that sound

The soundtrack of
my
Northern town

LITTLE MOSHER

Let's play little anarchists
and get dressed up today;
in tartan,
leather,
fishnets,
Docs;
let's mosh about
to nineties rock,
graffiti politics on toilet cubicles

And end up working
in insurance

SUNSHINE

Sometimes
you gotta be
your own
lover
Mother
significant other

Grab your own
outstretched hand,
pull yourself
up
and blink back
the water

Stand
a little taller

Smooth down
your crumpled clothes,
clench your trembling jaw
and stop staring down
at your shoes

at the floor

You don't belong
down
there

And don't let 'em tell you
you do
'cause they're wrong
they're wrong
they're wrong
they're all wrong

Lift your head
my love,
tilt it up to the sky

See that big yellow circle
hanging up high?

That's you

You are
sunshine

SUITS

When you were small
they told you "it's your life"
be an astronaut, musician, pilot
anything you like

But it's 6am
and your phone's beeping,
gotta be in early
for an 8am meeting

You wonder if Dolly Parton
started her nine to five
On the 7:15
TRAIN DELAYED
How many years until you're 65?

As you trudge down the platform
you all look the same,
umbrellas at the ready
for the Manchester rain

Suits and briefcases,
stocking-clad legs,
queues out the door
for Starbucks and Greggs

Crammed in lifts
like tinned sardines,
staring down
at smartphone screens

Black coffee in mugs
that try to be funny
'keep calm and carry on'
do you really need the money?

Fluorescent lighting,
clicking pens,
all caged in
like battery hens

"Does anyone have an agenda?"
does anyone really care?
"Any other business?"
this is a nightmare

Pie charts and numbers
up on a screen,
you smile and nod
but you just want to scream

Decades of living,
years in education,
and you're cornered in't kitchen
making polite conversation...

"Look at the weather"
"How was the train?"
you don't give a shit,
you're going insane

Every day
you seem to know
what everyone is having
for their tea when they're home

Someone said Darren
might be leaving his wife,
why are you so invested
in these people's lives?

From how many sugars
they have in their tea
to what's on offer
at their local Aldi

The names of their kids,
their team for the footie
and what colour sauce
they have on their butty

Keith's had a haircut,
Dave's got a new tie
What are you doing?
What is your life?

Acronyms and
business speak
"Blue sky thinking"
makes you seethe

"We're in the weeds,
let's car park that idea,
let's take it offline"
you need a fucking beer

You imagine them all
unzipping their skin
and stepping out of their suits,
humans within

And they'll talk like normal people
and their eyes will light up,
like they do Friday lunchtime
when they're down at the pub

EMOTIONAL HOARDER

Your mind is like
an Ikea showroom,
mine is like
my Grandma's attic,
you only keep what you need,
organised in perfect order,
I keep hold of everything,
I am an emotional hoarder

You throw away
what's old or broken
or doesn't match
your colour scheme,
I keep everything
regardless,
a jumbled mess
without a theme

You spring clean
and neatly label
boxes that all serve
a purpose,
I sift through dust
until i'm able
to pull old bin bags
to the surface

Filled with keepsakes
I should have thrown out
years ago
and let them go

Like you did

ANXIETY

The world ends
with every misconstrued word,
bAdly strung together sentence,
slip of the tongue

The world ends
with every misjudged movemeNt,
unintentional insult,
poorly timed kiss

The world ends
with every miXed message,
clumsy fumble,
awkward stumble

The world ends
wIth every misunderstood joke,
uncomfortable silence,
awkward elbow

The world Ends
with every missed opportunity,
unspoken word,
unrequited love

The world ends
with every misinTerpretation,
lack of understanding,
failure to comprehend

The world ends
with every bated breath,
sweatY palm,
knotted stomach

The world is filled with
Why?
How?
What if...

and it ends
every day

and then begins
again

SISTER

No one kept our bedrooms
as nostalgia shrines;
emotions sealed in
like sandwiches in
zip locked bags,
trapped
in time

They didn't have
the space,
ability
or stability

'Going Home for a few days'
is me lounging on yer corner sofa
and you mothering me
like i'm one of yer own

NEURODIVERSITY

A spreadsheet is never going to
reorganise the chaos in my brain
the very suggestion
is somewhat insane

A list is never going to
fix
this mess
inside my head

Practicality and positivity
are not medication
for my ADHD
and your inspirational quote
isn't gonna turn down the volume
or lower the pitch
it's not gonna
scratch
this itch

It won't cancel out the noise
or stop
the static
so you can keep it
and i'll just manage
this manic

Green tea
and meditation
aren't a massive
revelation
they're both
bloody ancient
been going 'round for
generations

So stop acting like
you're doing me
a favour
like you're some sort of
mental health saviour
by making these suggestions
on how to improve my behaviour

My behaviour
my behaviour
my
behaviour

Like it's a choice
like I wake up in the morning
and switch on that voice
in my mind
that never stops going

to let me unwind
that makes me distracted
when i'm trying to focus
that screams so loud

brain cell
hocus pocus

My mind is
a busy roundabout
with too many traffic lights
and too many signs
and too many junctions
for me to decide
what to do and
where to begin
and the car won't start
the engine's packed in
and I don't have a license
I can't even drive
i'm in the wrong lane
not sure how to
make it out
alive

So thanks for the pointers
and the tricks and tips
that i've already read up on
and tried
and then quit
'cause your spreadsheets are boring
and your green tea tastes likes crap
so i'll stick with my neurodiversity
and just
try
not to
crash

SELF-CARE

We run baths,
light candles,
drink herbal tea
and call it self-care
as we
pick
ourselves apart,
piece by piece,
wondering why we never feel
whole

DAYS

There's days when i'm empty
like,
the bottom of the barrell,
a scooped out
smashed up
avocado,
the kind you
might have on toast
for yer dinner,
spread reyt thin

Thin,
thin,
thinner

I am hollowed out
like a pumpkin rotting
in November,
my head's a mess
and I can't remember
how I felt without
a fake grin
carved in,
spitting seeds
and
swatting flies,
well past my sell by date,
rotting on't step outside

There's them kinda days

There's days when i'm filling up
and everything feels alright,
not horrible or spectacular,
Just ordinary,
nice

I'm hovering on a see saw
somewhere in't middle,
horizontal,
Inbetween

There's days like that

Then there's days when i'm full like
bursting to't brim,
glass overflowing,
so much of me
you could take a swim
in't overflow

down me in pints
for instant hydration,
make a splash in my waves,
let me be your vacation

There's them kinda days

Then there's days when i'm all three,
I'm everything, me

A walk on the beach,
my breath held under't sea

A hug from a lover,
hours spent sobbing under't covers

Bright blue sky
and
rolling thunder

I'm up, up, up!

Then i'm down,
going under

TOO BUSY LISTENING

There's piles of washing, Mum,
but i'm feeling fresh anyway

The bin should have gone out, Mum,
the day before Yesterday

I'm reminding myself not to get stressed
I'm embracing the chaos and accepting the mess

There's dirt on the laminate, Mum,
but my self esteem is glistening

There's pots in the sink, Mum,
we were too busy listening

to music, each other, the rain on the window
I'm learning to enjoy things, to just chill, and let go

The light bulbs need changing, Mum,
but my glow doesn't dim

There's not much in the cupboards, Mum,
but my heart is full to the brim

We've been cooking up laughter, connection and understanding
so I'm ignoring the cobwebs up on the landing

SIDE BY SIDE

The first thing I look at
and really **see**
after the hospital
climbing out of the car

Is them two chairs

Sitting side by side
in't front yard
green, sun-bleached plastic
one for you and one for her

They're both still there,
even though you're not

When I visit,
I sit on the wall

KARAOKE GRANDAD: SIDE A

You were obsessed with karaoke
shelves of books
handwritten lyrics
in your military cursive
a sea of cassettes
all perfectly labelled
in alphabetical order
you time stamped every recording

Testing testing one two three
every time I came round for tea
in your attic
where me Mam used to sleep
you'd tell me
when she was small like me

Grandchild
one of so many
I lost count
"Yeah he's me cousin
she is too"
it never stopped
just grew and grew

Not one of us
could fucking sing
all tone death
if anything

Me Sister sang
Everything I do I do it for you
and it were true
'cause you did
and I was **Three steps to heaven**
Viva Espana
It's my party and I'll cry if I want to
Daydream believer
and I always sang the word
Instrumental
And you were
Will you still love me tomorrow
and I always did
followed by
You were always on my mind
and you are
finished off with
Top of the world
and I aren't religious
but that's where
I think of you
now

And we laughed when you'd pop round to ours
every now and again
with a cassette of you
singing all your tunes
impeccably labelled
Benny '98

And I've got a walkman, Grandad

I listen to you sometimes
and I forgot you had a lisp
and how when you'd mess up you'd say
"start again Ben"
And it brings a tear to my eye
every time
'cause you're singing my life

Red red wine
Greatest love of all
Never be anyone else
Poetry in motion

Instrumental
Instrumental
Instrumental

KARAOKE GRANDAD: SIDE B

I think of you when
It's **Saturday night** and I'm **at the movies**
or when I walk the streets of Manchester
listening to **The rhythm of the rain**

When times are good
and I feel like it's a **Wonderful world**
I swear I can see you
on the corner of any and every road

Pulling up in your
blue Volvo
packed full of grandkids
you were **King of the road**

We were two to a seatbelt
and the little ones sat in't boot
fingers sticky from
jam butties and orange juice

Ducking down
when police cars passed
as you blasted out
The Carpenters

(and explained to us that health and safety
is just for people with no common sense)

And I know fuck all
about *history, biology,* or the *French I took*
but I do know
how to make a belting roll up
and pour a cracking pint
of Guinness
and I reckon you'd have preferred that
to be honest

And I swear
I can feel ya **Stand by me**
when I'm **Sitting on the dock of the…**
Pier
'cause I live in Wigan
and there's no bays here

And in answer to your question
all those years ago
yeah Grandad
I'll **Save the last dance for** you

SPOONS

I leave yer house with spoons
pressed into the palm of my hand,
with baking instructions
that I don't understand

The one with the red handle
that's meant for making pie,
I eat my cereal with it
every morning at nine

The little white porcelain one
is for measuring yeast
or summat to do with baking bread
but I used it to stir my tea

And I think
It's better that way
'cause it reminds me of you
at least five times a day

We take what we're given
and make it our own
like your Irish sense of humour
and strength of Yorkshire stone

BROKEN BISCUITS

When I visited as a kid
you'd always bring out
a big blue bag of
broken biscuits

and i'd sit at your kitchen table
trying to put them back together again
saying "I can fix them all Gran"
but I couldn't

and I can't

WE ARE ALL FRAGMENTS OF SOMEBODY ELSE

I am rolling hills
and purple heather,
towering mills
and get-togethers

I am a working men's club
where, at age five
I slid on my knees across the dancefloor
and ruined my tights

Where balloons float on't floor
or hang limply from lighting fixtures
because my Grandad thinks helium
is a 'bloody rip off'

My Dad is unashamedly first to the buffet
for pies, quiche and egg mayo,
Yorkshire-style nineties tapas,
topped off with my Grandma's gateau

He tells me my eyes
are bigger than my belly
but I eat a whole paper plate worth
with room still for jelly

We are all fragments of somebody else

I am crawling under trestle tables,
sifting through the streamers from party poppers,

flicking aside the cardboard bits
on my hunt for drunkenly dropped coppers

I am badly singing karaoke as
my Grandad shares his microphone,
his fingers wrapped around it
are identical to my own

We are all fragments of somebody else

I am four years old
napping under my parents' coats
wi' a belly full of bombay mix
and full fat coke

Us kids top and tail on the same booth bench,
rosy cheeks sticking to't dark green leather,
in and out of brightly-lit, disco ball dreams
as our parents do the Time Warp together

and my Mam dances
just a little out of time,
coordination I now recognise,
cautious, always one step behind

We are all fragments of somebody else

I am underage, drinking underpriced beer,
blowing smoke clouds up over't hills

perched on a toilet seat with my head out the window,
looking out at where my Grandma worked down at the mills

I am patterned carpets,
brightly lit bars,
taxi home past midnight and
walking down in't morning for't cars

Plastic cutlery and party dresses,
making memories and learning lessons,
one pound fifty spirits and mixers,
vol-au-vents and chicken dippers

Frankie Valli and the Four
generations